Church Episcopal

Family prayers for the Christian year

Church Episcopal

Family prayers for the Christian year

ISBN/EAN: 9783337283728

Printed in Europe, USA, Canada, Australia, Japan

Cover: Foto ©Lupo / pixelio.de

More available books at **www.hansebooks.com**

Family Prayers for The Christian Year

ARRANGED BY

WM. A. SNIVELY, D.D.

SECOND EDITION

NEW-YORK
THOMAS WHITTAKER
2 & 3 BIBLE HOUSE

Contents.

	PAGE
SEASONS OF THE CHRISTIAN YEAR	vii
A TABLE OF THE MOVEABLE FEASTS	ix
A TABLE OF THE IMMOVEABLE FEASTS	xi
A TABLE OF FASTS	xiii
MORNING PRAYER	3
EVENING PRAYER	8
THE LITANY	13
THE PSALTER	19
THE COLLECTS	35
OCCASIONAL PRAYERS	159
GRACE AT TABLE	191
THE BEATITUDES OF THE GOSPEL	193
THE SUMMARY OF THE LAW	197
EVEN SONG	201

Seasons of the Christian Year.

	PAGE
Advent	37
Christmastide	43
Epiphany	53
Pre-Lenten Season	63
Lent	69
Eastertide	85
Ascensiontide	97
Whitsuntide	101
Trinity	107

A Table of the Moveable Feasts.

The year of our Lord.	Sundays after Epiphany.	Septuagesima Sunday.	Ash-Wednesday.	Easter-Day.	Ascension-Day.	Whitsun-Day.	Sundays after Trinity.	Advent Sunday.
1888	3	Jan. 29	Feb. 15	Apr. 1	May 10	May 20	26	Dec. 2
1889	5	Feb. 17	Mar. 6	Apr. 21	May 30	June 9	23	Dec. 1
1890	3	Feb. 2	Feb. 19	Apr. 6	May 15	May 25	25	Nov. 30
1891	2	Jan. 25	Feb. 11	Mar. 29	May 7	May 17	26	Nov. 29
1892	5	Feb. 14	Mar. 2	Apr. 17	May 26	June 5	23	Nov. 27
1893	3	Jan. 29	Feb. 15	Apr. 2	May 11	May 21	26	Dec. 3
1894	2	Jan. 21	Feb. 7	Mar. 25	May 3	May 13	27	Dec. 2
1895	4	Feb. 10	Feb. 27	Apr. 14	May 23	June 2	24	Dec. 1
1896	3	Feb. 2	Feb. 19	Apr. 5	May 14	May 24	25	Nov. 29
1897	5	Feb. 14	Mar. 3	Apr. 18	May 27	June 6	23	Nov. 28
1898	4	Feb. 6	Feb. 23	Apr. 10	May 19	May 29	24	Nov. 27
1899	3	Jan. 29	Feb. 15	Apr. 2	May 11	May 21	26	Dec. 3
1900	5	Feb. 11	Feb. 28	Apr. 15	May 24	June 3	24	Dec. 2

A Table of the Immoveable Feasts.

ALL SUNDAYS IN THE YEAR.

		PAGE
Nov. 30	St. Andrew	137
Dec. 21	St. Thomas	138
Dec. 25	Christmas-day	43
Dec. 26	St. Stephen	47
Dec. 27	St. John, Evangelist	48
Dec. 28	Holy Innocents	49
Jan. 1	Circumcision	51
Jan. 6	Epiphany	53
Jan. 25	Conversion St. Paul	139
Feb. 2	Purification B. V. M.	140
Feb. 24	St. Matthias	141
Mar. 25	Annunciation B. V. M.	142
Apr. 25	St. Mark	143
May 1	St. Philip and St. James	144
June 11	St. Barnabas	145
June 24	St. John Baptist	146
June 29	St. Peter	147
July 25	St. James	148
Aug. 6	The Transfiguration of Christ	149
Aug. 24	St. Bartholomew	150
Sept. 21	St. Matthew	151
Sept. 29	St. Michael and all Angels	152
Oct. 18	St. Luke the Evangelist	153
Oct. 28	St. Simon and St. Jude	154
Nov. 1	All Saints	155
	Thanksgiving-day	156

Table of Fasts.

ASH-WEDNESDAY. Page 71
GOOD FRIDAY. " 82

✠

Days of Abstinence.

THE FORTY DAYS OF LENT.

THE EMBER DAYS. Page 157

Wednesday,
Friday, } after the first Sunday in Lent.
Saturday,

Wednesday,
Friday, } after the Feast of Pentecost.
Saturday,

Wednesday,
Friday, } after September Fourteenth.
Saturday,

Wednesday,
Friday, } after December Thirteenth.
Saturday,

THE THREE ROGATION DAYS. Page 158

Monday,
Tuesday, } before Holy Thursday, or the Ascension of our Lord.
Wednesday,

ALL THE FRIDAYS IN THE YEAR EXCEPT CHRISTMAS-DAY.

Morning and Evening Prayers.

The service may begin with a Lesson from Holy Scripture or with the proper Sentence for the Day. The use of the Psalter is optional. If omitted, the Lesson or the Sentence for the Day may be used instead: but the Gloria Patri should always be said whether the Psalter is used or not.

Morning Prayer.

All standing up, the Reader shall say:

V. In the Name of the Father, and of the Son, and of the Holy Ghost.
R. Amen.
V. I laid me down and slept, and rose up again; for the Lord sustained me.
R. Thanks be to Thee, O Lord.
V. Praise ye the Lord.
R. The Lord's Name be praised.

Here may be used the Psalm for the Day [vid. pages 19-34], concluding with

The Gloria Patri.

GLORY be to the Father, and to the Son, and to the Holy Ghost;
R. As it was in the beginning, is now, and ever shall be, world without end. Amen.

Then shall be said

The Apostles' Creed.

I BELIEVE in God the Father Almighty, Maker of heaven and earth: And in Jesus Christ his only Son, our Lord; Who was conceived by the Holy Ghost, Born of the Virgin Mary; Suffered under Pontius Pilate, Was crucified, dead, and buried; He descended into hell, The third day he rose again from the dead; He ascended into heaven, And sitteth on the right hand of God the Father Almighty; From thence he shall come to judge the quick and the dead.

I believe in the Holy Ghost; The holy Catholic Church; The Communion of Saints; The Forgiveness of sins; The Resurrection of the body; And the Life everlasting. Amen.

> And after that, these Prayers following, all devoutly kneeling: the Reader first pronouncing,

V. The Lord be with you.
R. And with thy spirit.

Let us pray.

V. O Lord, show Thy mercy upon us;
R. And grant us Thy salvation.
V. O God, make clean our hearts within us;
R. And take not Thy Holy Spirit from us.
V. O God, make speed to save us.
R. O Lord, make haste to help us.

The Lord's Prayer.

OUR Father, who art in heaven, Hallowed be Thy Name. Thy kingdom come. Thy will be done on earth, As it is in heaven. Give us this day our daily bread. And forgive us our trespasses, As we forgive those who trespass against us. And lead us not into temptation; But deliver us from evil: For Thine is the kingdom, and the power, and the glory, for ever and ever. Amen.

> Then shall be said the Collect for the Day, and afterward these prayers, with any special prayers appropriate to the occasion.

A Collect for Peace.

O GOD, who art the author of peace and lover of concord, in knowledge of whom standeth our eternal life, whose service is perfect freedom; Defend us Thy humble servants in all assaults of our enemies; that we, surely trusting in Thy defence, may not fear the power of any adversaries, through the might of Jesus Christ our Lord. *Amen.*

A Collect for Grace.

O LORD, our heavenly Father, Almighty and everlasting God, who hast safely brought us to the beginning of this day; Defend us in the same with Thy mighty power; and grant that this day we fall into no sin, neither run into any kind of danger; but that all our doings, being ordered by Thy governance, may be righteous in Thy sight; through Jesus Christ our Lord. *Amen.*

V. O Lord, show Thou us the way that we should walk in ;
R. For we lift up our souls unto Thee.
V. Hold Thou up our goings in Thy paths ;
R. That our footsteps slip not.

> On Wednesdays and Fridays the Litany [vid. page 15] may be used here.

2 *Cor.* 13 : 14.

THE grace of our Lord Jesus Christ, and the love of God, and the fellowship of the Holy Ghost, be with us all evermore. *Amen.*

Evening Prayer.

All standing up, the Reader shall say:

V. In the Name of the Father, and of the Son, and of the Holy Ghost.

R. Amen.

V. I will lay me down in peace, and take my rest.

R. For it is Thou, Lord, only that makest me dwell in safety.

V. Let my prayer be set forth in Thy sight as the incense:

R. And the lifting up of my hands as an evening sacrifice.

V. Praise ye the Lord.

R. The Lord's Name be praised.

Here may follow the Psalm for the Day [pp. 19-34], concluding with

The Gloria Patri.

GLORY be to the Father, and to the Son, and to the Holy Ghost;

R. As it was in the beginning, is now, and ever shall be, world without end. Amen.

Then shall be said

The Apostles' Creed.

I BELIEVE in God the Father Almighty, Maker of heaven and earth: And in Jesus Christ his only Son, our Lord; Who was conceived by the Holy Ghost, Born of the Virgin Mary; Suffered under Pontius Pilate, Was crucified, dead, and buried; He descended into hell, The third day he rose again from the dead; He ascended into heaven, And sitteth on the right hand of God the Father Almighty; From thence he shall come to judge the quick and the dead.

I believe in the Holy Ghost; The holy Catholic Church; The Communion of Saints; The forgiveness of sins; The Resurrection of the body; And the Life everlasting. Amen.

> And after that, these Prayers following, all devoutly kneeling: the Reader first pronouncing.

V. The Lord be with you.
R. And with thy spirit.

Let us pray.

V. O Lord, show Thy mercy upon us;

R. And grant us Thy salvation.

V. O God, make clean our hearts within us;

R. And take not Thy Holy Spirit from us.

V. O God, make speed to save us.

R. O Lord, make haste to help us.

The Lord's Prayer.

OUR Father, who art in heaven, Hallowed be Thy Name. Thy kingdom come. Thy will be done on earth, As it is in heaven. Give us this day our daily bread. And forgive us our trespasses, As we forgive those who trespass against us. And lead us not into temptation; But deliver us from evil: For Thine is the kingdom, and the power, and the glory, for ever and ever. Amen.

Then shall be said the Collect for the Day, and after that, the Collects following, with any special prayers appropriate to the occasion.

A Collect for Peace.

O GOD, from whom all holy desires, all good counsels, and all just works do proceed, Give unto Thy servants that peace which the world cannot give; that our hearts may be set to obey Thy commandments, and also that by Thee, we, being defended from the fear of our enemies, may pass our time in rest and quietness; through the merits of Jesus Christ our Saviour. *Amen.*

A Collect for Aid against Perils.

LIGHTEN our darkness we beseech Thee, O Lord, and by Thy great mercy defend us from all perils and dangers of this night; for the love of Thy only Son, our Saviour, Jesus Christ. *Amen.*

V. So teach us to number our days,
R. That we may apply our hearts unto wisdom.
V. The Lord Almighty grant us a quiet night and a rest from toil.
R. Amen.

2 *Cor.* 13:14.

THE grace of our Lord Jesus Christ, and the love of God, and the fellowship of the Holy Ghost, be with us all evermore. *Amen.*

The Litany.

The Litany.

¶ To be used on Wednesdays and Fridays, after the Versicles in the Morning Service.

O GOD the Father of Heaven; have mercy upon us miserable sinners.
O God the Father of Heaven; have mercy upon us miserable sinners.
O God the Son, Redeemer of the world; have mercy upon us miserable sinners.
O God the Son, Redeemer of the World; have mercy upon us miserable sinners.
O God the Holy Ghost, proceeding from the Father and the Son; have mercy upon us miserable sinners.

O God the Holy Ghost, proceeding from the Father and the Son ; have mercy upon us miserable sinners.

O holy, blessed, and glorious Trinity, three Persons and one God; have mercy upon us miserable sinners.

O holy, blessed, and glorious Trinity, three Persons and one God; have mercy upon us miserable sinners.

Remember not, Lord, our offences nor the offences of our forefathers; neither take Thou vengeance of our sins: spare us, good Lord, spare Thy people, whom Thou hast redeemed with Thy most precious blood, and be not angry with us for ever.

Spare us, good Lord.

Son of God, we beseech Thee to hear us.

Son of God, we beseech Thee to hear us.

O Lamb of God, who takest away the sins of the world;

Grant us Thy peace.

O Lamb of God, who takest away the sins of the world;
Have mercy upon us.

Let us pray.

WE humbly beseech Thee, O Father, mercifully to look upon our infirmities; and, for the glory of Thy Name, turn from us all those evils that we most justly have deserved; and grant, that in all our troubles, we may put our whole trust and confidence in Thy mercy, and evermore serve Thee in holiness and pureness of living, to Thy honor and glory; through our only Mediator and Advocate, Jesus Christ our LORD. *Amen.*

The Psalter.

The Psalter.

Sunday Morning.

THIS is the day which the LORD hath made;
We will rejoice and be glad in it.
The LORD loveth the gates of Zion;
More than all the dwellings of Jacob.
I was glad when they said unto me;
We will go into the House of the LORD.
I will wash my hands in innocency, O LORD;
And so will I go to Thine altar.
The LORD hath chosen Zion;
He hath desired it for His habitation.
I will also clothe her priests with salvation,
And her saints shall shout aloud for joy.
GLORIA PATRI.

Sunday Evening.

O GIVE thanks unto the LORD, for He is good;
For His mercy endureth for ever.
Surely His salvation is nigh them that fear Him;
That glory may dwell in our land.
Truth shall spring out of the earth;
And righteousness shall look down from heaven.
Yea, the LORD shall give us that which is good,
And our land shall yield her increase.
Righteousness shall go before Him;
And shall set us in the way of His steps.

GLORIA PATRI.

Monday Morning.

MY voice shalt Thou hear betimes, O Lord;
Early in the morning will I direct my prayer unto Thee.
The Lord is nigh unto all that call upon Him;
To all that call upon Him in truth.
He will fulfill the desire of them that fear Him;
He also will hear their cry, and will save them.
My mouth shall speak the praise of the Lord,
And let all flesh bless His holy Name for ever.

Gloria Patri.

Monday Evening.

T HOU knowest my down-sitting and mine up-rising;
Thou understandest my thoughts long before.
Thou art about my path and about my bed;
And spiest out all my ways.
If I say, Peradventure the darkness shall cover me;
Then shall my night be turned to day.
Yea, the darkness is no darkness with Thee.
But the night is as clear as the day.

Gloria Patri.

Tuesday Morning.

THE righteous cry and the LORD heareth;
And delivereth them out of all their troubles.
The LORD is nigh unto them that are of a broken heart,
And saveth such as be of a contrite spirit;
Many are the afflictions of the righteous;
But the LORD delivereth him out of them all.
The LORD redeemeth the soul of His servants;
And none of them that trust in Him shall be desolate.

GLORIA PATRI.

Tuesday Evening.

How dear are Thy counsels unto me, O God;
O how great is the sum of them:
If I tell them, they are more in number than the sand;
When I wake up, I am present with Thee.
Try me, O God, and seek the ground of my heart;
Prove me and examine my thoughts;
Look well if there be any way of wickedness in me,
And lead me in the way everlasting.

GLORIA PATRI.

Wednesday Morning.

I WILL lift up mine eyes unto the hills,
From whence cometh my help.
My help cometh even from the LORD,
Who hath made heaven and earth.
The LORD himself is thy keeper;
The LORD is thy defence upon thy right hand.
The LORD shall preserve thee from all evil;
Yea, it is even He that shall keep thy soul.

GLORIA PATRI.

Wednesday Evening.

THE heavens declare the glory of God;
And the firmament sheweth His handiwork.
The law of the Lord is an undefiled law, converting the soul;
The testimony of the Lord is sure and giveth wisdom unto the simple.
The statutes of the Lord are right and rejoice the heart;
The commandment of the Lord is pure, and giveth light unto the eyes.
The fear of the Lord is clean and endureth forever;
The judgments of the Lord are true, and righteous altogether.

Gloria Patri.

Thursday Morning.

O MAGNIFY the Lord with me,
And let us exalt His Name together.
I sought the Lord, and He heard me,
And delivered me from all my fears.
O taste and see that the Lord is good;
Blessed is the man that trusteth in Him.
O give thanks unto the Lord, for he is gracious;
Because His mercy endureth forever.

GLORIA PATRI.

Thursday Evening.

BE THOU my Judge, O Lord, for I have walked innocently;
My trust hath been also in the Lord, therefore shall I not fall.
Examine me, O Lord, and prove me;
Try out my reins and my heart.
For Thy loving-kindness is ever before mine eyes,
And I will walk in Thy Truth.
Give me understanding, and I shall keep Thy law;
Yea, I shall keep it with my whole heart.

Gloria Patri.

Friday Morning.

BLESSED is he whose unrighteousness is forgiven,
And whose sin is covered.
Blessed is the man unto whom the LORD imputeth no sin;
And in whose spirit there is no guile.
I will acknowledge my sin unto Thee,
And mine unrighteousness have I not hid.
I said, I will confess my sins unto the LORD;
And so Thou forgavest the wickedness of my sin.

GLORIA PATRI.

Friday Evening.

HIDE Thy face from my sins;
    And blot out all mine iniquities.
Create in me a clean heart, O God,
And renew a right spirit within me.
Cast me not away from Thy presence,
And take not Thy Holy Spirit from me.
Restore unto me the joy of Thy salvation,
And uphold me with Thy free Spirit.

GLORIA PATRI.

Saturday Morning.

IN THEE, O Lord, have I put my trust,
Let me never be put to confusion.
Thou, Lord, art the thing that I long for,
Thou art my hope even from my youth.
O let my mouth be filled with Thy praise,
That I may sing of Thy glory and honor all the day long.
Hold Thou me up and I shall be safe;
Yea, my delight shall be ever in Thy statutes.

   Gloria Patri.

Saturday Evening.

LORD, I have loved the habitation of Thy house;
And the place where Thine honor dwelleth.
Hearken unto my voice when I cry unto Thee;
Have mercy upon me and hear me.
O hide not Thou Thy face from me;
Nor cast Thy servant away in displeasure:
For Thy loving-kindness is ever before mine eyes,
And I will walk in Thy Truth.

    GLORIA PATRI.

The Collects for
The Sundays and Holy Days
Throughout the Year.

The Sentence may be used daily instead of the Lesson or the Psalter, or as an Antiphon preceding the Creed, at the discretion of the Reader.

Advent.

The Collects.

TO BE USED THROUGHOUT THE YEAR.

The First Sunday in Advent.

The Collect.

ALMIGHTY God, give us grace that we may cast away the works of darkness, and put upon us the armor of light, now in the time of this mortal life, in which Thy Son Jesus Christ came to visit us in great humility; that in the last day, when He shall come again in His glorious Majesty to judge both the quick and dead, we may rise to the life immortal, through Him who liveth and reigneth with Thee and the Holy Ghost now and ever. *Amen.*

The Sentence.

THE night is far spent, the day is at hand: let us therefore cast off the works of darkness, and let us put on the armor of light. *Rom.* 13 : 12.

The Second Sunday in Advent.

The Collect.

BLESSED Lord, who hast caused all holy Scriptures to be written for our learning; Grant that we may in such wise hear them, read, mark, learn, and inwardly digest them, that by patience, and comfort of Thy holy Word, we may embrace, and ever hold fast the blessed hope of everlasting life, which Thou hast given us in our Saviour Jesus Christ. *Amen.*

The Sentence.

WHATSOEVER things were written aforetime were written for our learning, that we through patience and comfort of the Scriptures might have hope. *Rom.* 15:4.

The Third Sunday in Advent.

The Collect.

O LORD Jesus Christ, who at Thy first coming didst send Thy messenger to prepare Thy way before Thee; Grant that the ministers and stewards of Thy mysteries may likewise so prepare and make ready Thy way, by turning the hearts of the disobedient to the wisdom of the just, that at Thy second coming to judge the world we may be found an acceptable people in Thy sight, who livest and reignest with the Father and the Holy Spirit, ever one God, world without end. *Amen.*

The Sentence.

LET a man so account of us, as of the ministers of Christ, and stewards of the mysteries of God. 1 *Cor.* 4:1.

The Fourth Sunday in Advent.

The Collect.

O LORD, raise up, we pray Thee, Thy power, and come among us, and with great might succor us; that whereas, through our sins and wickedness, we are sore let and hindered in running the race that is set before us, Thy bountiful grace and mercy may speedily help and deliver us; through the satisfaction of Thy Son our Lord, to whom, with Thee and the Holy Ghost, be honor and glory, world without end. *Amen.*

The Sentence.

THE peace of God, which passeth all understanding, shall keep your hearts and minds through Christ Jesus.
Phil. 4:7.

Christmas.

The Nativity of our Lord, or the Birth-day of Christ, commonly called Christmas-day.

The Collect.

ALMIGHTY God, who hast given us Thy only-begotten Son to take our nature upon Him, and as at this time to be born of a pure virgin; Grant that we being regenerate, and made Thy children by adoption and grace, may daily be renewed by Thy Holy Spirit; through the same our Lord Jesus Christ, who liveth and reigneth with Thee and the same Spirit, ever one God, world without end. *Amen.*

The Sentence.

FOR unto you is born this day in the city of David a Saviour, which is Christ the LORD. *St. Luke* 2:11.

The Nativity of our Lord, or the Birth-day of Christ, commonly called Christmas-day.

The Second Collect.

O GOD, who makest us glad with the yearly remembrance of the birth of Thine only Son Jesus Christ; Grant that as we joyfully receive Him for our Redeemer, so we may with sure confidence behold Him, when He shall come to be our Judge, who liveth and reigneth, with Thee and the Holy Ghost, one God, world without end. *Amen.*

The Sentence.

GLORY to God in the highest, and on earth peace, good will towards men. *St. Luke* 2:14.

Saint Stephen's Day
(December 26).

The Collect.

GRANT, O LORD, that, in all our sufferings here upon earth for the testimony of Thy truth, we may steadfastly look up to heaven, and by faith behold the glory that shall be revealed; and, being filled with the Holy Ghost, may learn to love and bless our persecutors by the example of Thy first martyr Saint Stephen, who prayed for his murderers to Thee, O blessed Jesus, who standest at the right hand of God to succor all those who suffer for Thee, our only Mediator and Advocate. *Amen.*

The Sentence.

AND he kneeled down, and cried with a loud voice, LORD, lay not this sin to their charge. And when he had said this, he fell asleep. *Acts* 7 : 60.

Saint John the Evangelist's Day
(December 27).

The Collect.

MERCIFUL Lord, we beseech Thee to cast Thy bright beams of light upon Thy Church, that it being instructed by the doctrine of Thy blessed Apostle and Evangelist Saint John, may so walk in the light of Thy truth, that it may at length attain to everlasting life; through Jesus Christ our Lord. *Amen.*

The Sentence.

IF we walk in the light, as He is in the light, we have fellowship one with another, and the blood of Jesus Christ His Son cleanseth us from all sin.

1 *St. John* 1:7.

The Innocents' Day
(December 28).

The Collect.

O ALMIGHTY God, who out of the mouths of babes and sucklings hast ordained strength, and madest infants to glorify Thee by their deaths; Mortify and kill all vices in us, and so strengthen us by Thy grace, that by the innocency of our lives, and constancy of our faith even unto death, we may glorify Thy holy Name; through Jesus Christ our Lord. *Amen.*

The Sentence.

OUT of the mouth of babes and sucklings hast Thou ordained strength.
Ps. 8:2.

The Sunday after Christmas-day.

The Collect.

ALMIGHTY God, who hast given us Thy only-begotten Son to take our nature upon Him, and as at this time to be born of a pure virgin; Grant that we, being regenerate, and made Thy children by adoption and grace, may daily be renewed by Thy Holy Spirit; through the same our Lord Jesus Christ, who liveth and reigneth with Thee and the same Spirit, ever one God, world without end. *Amen.*

The Sentence.

BEHOLD, I bring you good tidings of great joy, which shall be to all people. *St. Luke* 2 : 10.

The Circumcision of Christ
(January 1).

The Collect.

ALMIGHTY God, who madest Thy blessed Son to be circumcised, and obedient to the law for man; Grant us the true circumcision of the Spirit; that, our hearts, and all our members, being mortified from all worldly and carnal lusts, we may in all things obey Thy blessed will; through the same Thy Son Jesus Christ our Lord. *Amen.*

The Sentence.

AND when eight days were accomplished for the circumcising of the child, His name was called Jesus, which was so named of the angel before He was conceived in the womb. *St. Luke* 2:21.

Epiphany.

The Epiphany, or the Manifestation of Christ to the Gentiles (Jan. 6).

The Collect.

O GOD, who by the leading of a star didst manifest Thy only-begotten Son to the Gentiles; Mercifully grant that we, who know Thee now by faith, may after this life have the fruition of Thy glorious Godhead; through Jesus Christ our Lord. *Amen.*

The Sentence.

THE Gentiles shall come to Thy light, and kings to the brightness of Thy rising. *Isa.* 60 : 3.

The First Sunday after the Epiphany.

The Collect.

O LORD, we beseech Thee mercifully to receive the prayers of Thy people who call upon Thee; and grant that they may both perceive and know what things they ought to do, and also may have grace and power faithfully to fulfill the same; through Jesus Christ our Lord. *Amen.*

The Sentence.

FROM the rising of the sun even to the going down of the same my Name shall be great among the Gentiles.
Mal. 1:11.

The Second Sunday after the Epiphany.

The Collect.

ALMIGHTY and everlasting God, who dost govern all things in heaven and earth; Mercifully hear the supplications of Thy people, and grant us Thy peace all the days of our life; through Jesus Christ our Lord. *Amen.*

The Sentence.

GOD so loved the world, that He gave His only begotten Son, that whosoever believeth in Him should not perish, but have everlasting life.
St. John 3 : 16.

The Third Sunday after the Epiphany.

The Collect.

ALMIGHTY and everlasting God, mercifully look upon our infirmities, and in all our dangers and necessities stretch forth Thy right hand to help and defend us; through Jesus Christ our Lord. *Amen.*

The Sentence.

NOW therefore ye are no more strangers and foreigners, but fellow-citizens with the Saints, and of the household of God. *Eph.* 2:19.

The Fourth Sunday after the Epiphany.

The Collect.

O GOD, who knowest us to be set in the midst of so many and great dangers, that by reason of the frailty of our nature we cannot always stand upright; Grant to us such strength and protection, as may support us in all dangers, and carry us through all temptations; through Jesus Christ our Lord. *Amen.*

The Sentence.

THE men marvelled, saying, What manner of man is this, that even the winds and the sea obey Him!
St. Matt. 8 : 27.

The Fifth Sunday after the Epiphany.

The Collect.

O LORD, we beseech Thee to keep Thy Church and household continually in Thy true religion; that they who do lean only upon the hope of Thy heavenly grace may evermore be defended by Thy mighty power; through Jesus Christ our Lord. *Amen.*

The Sentence.

LET the word of Christ dwell in you richly in all wisdom. *Col.* 3:16.

The Sixth Sunday after the Epiphany.

The Collect.

O GOD, whose blessed Son was manifested that He might destroy the works of the devil, and make us the sons of God, and heirs of eternal life; Grant us, we beseech Thee, that, having this hope, we may purify ourselves, even as He is pure; that, when He shall appear again with power and great glory, we may be made like unto Him in His eternal and glorious kingdom; where, with Thee, O Father, and Thee, O Holy Ghost, He liveth and reigneth, ever one God, world without end. *Amen.*

The Sentence.

WE know that, when He shall appear, we shall be like Him; for we shall see Him as he is.

1 *St. John* 3:2.

Pre-Lenten Season.

The Sunday called Septuagesima, or the Third Sunday before Lent.

The Collect.

O LORD, we beseech Thee favorably to hear the prayers of Thy people; that we, who are justly punished for our offences, may be mercifully delivered by Thy goodness, for the glory of Thy Name; through Jesus Christ our Saviour, who liveth and reigneth with Thee and the Holy Ghost, ever one God, world without end. *Amen.*

The Sentence.

THE last shall be first, and the first last: for many be called, but few chosen. *St. Matt.* 20:16.

The Sunday called Sexagesima, or the Second Sunday before Lent.

The Collect.

O LORD God, who seest that we put not our trust in anything that we do; Mercifully grant that by Thy power we may be defended against all adversity; through Jesus Christ our Lord. *Amen.*

The Sentence.

BUT that on the good ground are they, which in an honest and good heart, having heard the word, keep it, and bring forth fruit with patience.

St. Luke 8 : 15.

The Sunday called Quinquagesima, or the Next Sunday before Lent.

The Collect.

O LORD, who hast taught us that all our doings without charity are nothing worth; Send Thy Holy Ghost, and pour into our hearts that most excellent gift of charity, the very bond of peace and of all virtues, without which whosoever liveth is counted dead before Thee. Grant this for Thine only Son Jesus Christ's sake. *Amen.*

The Sentence.

AND now abideth faith, hope, charity, these three; but the greatest of these is charity. 1 *Cor.* 13:13.

Lent.

The First Day of Lent, commonly called Ash Wednesday.

The Collect.

ALMIGHTY and everlasting God, who hatest nothing that Thou hast made, and dost forgive the sins of all those who are penitent; Create and make in us new and contrite hearts, that we worthily lamenting our sins, and acknowledging our wretchedness, may obtain of Thee, the God of all mercy, perfect remission and forgiveness; through Jesus Christ our Lord. *Amen.*

The Sentence.

THE sacrifices of God are a broken spirit: a broken and a contrite heart, O God, Thou wilt not despise.
Ps. 51 : 17.

The First Sunday in Lent.

The Collect.

O LORD, who for our sake didst fast forty days and forty nights; give us grace to use such abstinence, that, our flesh being subdued to the Spirit, we may ever obey Thy godly motions in righteousness, and true holiness, to Thy honor and glory, who livest and reignest with the Father and the Holy Ghost, one God, world without end. *Amen.*

The Sentence.

ENTER not into judgment with thy servant, O LORD; for in thy sight shall no man living be justified.

Ps. 143:2.

The Second Sunday in Lent.

The Collect.

ALMIGHTY God, who seest that we have no power of ourselves to help ourselves; Keep us both outwardly in our bodies, and inwardly in our souls; that we may be defended from all adversities which may happen to the body, and from all evil thoughts which may assault and hurt the soul; through Jesus Christ our Lord. *Amen.*

The Sentence.

WHEN the wicked man turneth away from his wickedness that he hath committed, and doeth that which is lawful and right, he shall save his soul alive. *Ezek.* 18 : 27.

The Third Sunday in Lent.

The Collect.

WE beseech Thee, Almighty God, look upon the hearty desires of Thy humble servants, and stretch forth the right hand of Thy Majesty, to be our defence against all our enemies; through Jesus Christ our Lord. *Amen.*

The Sentence.

TO the LORD our GOD belong mercies and forgivenesses, though we have rebelled against him; neither have we obeyed the voice of the LORD our GOD, to walk in his laws which he set before us. *Dan.* 9 : 9, 10.

The Fourth Sunday in Lent.

The Collect.

GRANT, we beseech thee, Almighty God, that we, who for our evil deeds do worthily deserve to be punished, by the comfort of Thy grace may mercifully be relieved; through our Lord and Saviour Jesus Christ. *Amen.*

The Sentence.

HIDE Thy face from my sins, and blot out all mine iniquities.
Ps. 51 : 9.

The Fifth Sunday in Lent.

The Collect.

WE beseech Thee, Almighty God, mercifully to look upon Thy people; that by Thy great goodness they may be governed and preserved evermore, both in body and soul; through Jesus Christ our Lord. *Amen.*

The Sentence.

FOR by one offering He hath perfected forever them that are sanctified. *Heb.* 10:14.

The Sunday Next before Easter.

The Collect.

ALMIGHTY and everlasting God, who, of Thy tender love towards mankind, has sent Thy Son, our Saviour Jesus Christ, to take upon Him our flesh, and to suffer death upon the cross, that all mankind should follow the example of His great humility; Mercifully grant, that we may both follow the example of His patience, and also be made partakers of His resurrection; through the same Jesus Christ our Lord. *Amen.*

The Sentence.

HE is despised and rejected of men; a man of sorrows, and acquainted with grief. *Isa.* 53:3.

Monday before Easter.

The Collect.

ALMIGHTY and everlasting God; Grant us so to celebrate the mysteries of our Lord's Passion, that we, obtaining pardon through His precious Blood, may come with joy to the commemoration of that sacrifice by which Thou hast been pleased to redeem us; through the same Thy Son our Saviour Jesus Christ. *Amen.*

The Sentence.

SURELY He hath borne our griefs, and carried our sorrows: yet we did esteem Him stricken, smitten of God and afflicted. *Isa.* 53:4.

Tuesday before Easter.

The Collect.

O LORD God, whose blessed Son our Saviour gave His back to the smiters, and did not hide His face from shame; Grant us grace to take joyfully the sufferings of the present time, in full assurance of the glory that shall be revealed; through the same Jesus Christ our Lord. *Amen.*

The Sentence.

I GAVE my back to the smiters, and my cheeks to them that plucked off the hair: I hid not my face from shame and spitting. *Isa.* 50:6.

Wednesday before Easter.

The Collect.

MERCIFUL Father, give us grace that we never presume to sin through the example of a fellow-creature; but if we be led at any time to offend Thy Divine Majesty, vouchsafe us to repent with Peter, rather than to despair with Judas, so that by a godly sorrow and a lively faith we may obtain remission of our sins; through the only merits of Thy Son, Christ our Lord. *Amen.*

The Sentence.

BUT now once in the end of the world hath He appeared to put away sin by the sacrifice of Himself.

Heb. 9 : 26.

Thursday before Easter.

The Collect.

ALMIGHTY Father, whose dear Son did in the Garden of Gethsemane accept the cup Thou gavest Him to drink, that so He might taste death for every man; Mercifully grant that we to whom He ministers the cup of blessing may thankfully receive it in remembrance of Him, and show our Lord's death till He come; who liveth and reigneth with Thee and the Holy Ghost, one God, world without end.
Amen.

The Sentence.

FOR as often as ye eat this bread, and drink this cup, ye do shew the LORD's death until He come.
1 *Cor.* 11:26.

Good Friday.

The Collects.

ALMIGHTY God, we beseech Thee graciously to behold this Thy family, for which our LORD JESUS CHRIST was contented to be betrayed, and given up into the hands of wicked men, and to suffer death upon the cross, who now liveth and reigneth with Thee and the Holy Ghost, ever one God, world without end. *Amen.*

ALMIGHTY and everlasting God, by whose Spirit the whole body of the Church is governed and sanctified; Receive our supplications and prayers, which we offer before Thee for all estates of men in Thy holy Church, that every member of the same, in his vocation and ministry, may truly and godly serve Thee; through our Lord and Saviour Jesus Christ. *Amen.*

Good Friday.

The Collects.

O MERCIFUL God, who hast made all men, and hatest nothing that Thou hast made, nor desirest the death of a sinner, but rather that he should be converted and live; Have mercy upon all Jews, Turks, Infidels, and Heretics; and take from them all ignorance, hardness of heart, and contempt of Thy word; and so fetch them home, blessed Lord, to Thy flock, that they may be saved among the remnant of the true Israelites, and be made one fold under one Shepherd, Jesus Christ our Lord, who liveth and reigneth with Thee and the Holy Spirit, one God, world without end. *Amen.*

The Sentence.

HE said, It is finished: and He bowed His head, and gave up the ghost. *St. John* 19 : 30.

Easter-Even.

The Collect.

GRANT, O Lord, that as we are baptized into the death of Thy blessed Son our Saviour Jesus Christ, so by continual mortifying our corrupt affections we may be buried with Him; and that through the grave, and gate of death, we may pass to our joyful resurrection; for His merits, who died, and was buried, and rose again for us, Thy Son Jesus Christ our Lord. *Amen.*

The Sentence.

AND when Joseph had taken the body, he wrapped it in a clean linen cloth, and laid it in his own new tomb, which he had hewn out in the rock. *St. Matt.* 27:59, 60.

Easter.

Easter Day.

The Collect.

ALMIGHTY God, who through Thine only begotten Son Jesus Christ hast overcome death, and opened unto us the gate of everlasting life; We humbly beseech Thee, that, as by Thy special grace preventing us Thou dost put into our minds good desires, so by Thy continual help we may bring the same to good effect; through Jesus Christ our Lord, who liveth and reigneth with Thee and the Holy Ghost, ever one God, world without end. *Amen.*

The Sentence.

NOW is Christ risen from the dead, and become the first-fruits of them that slept. 1 *Cor.* 15:20.

Easter-Day.

The Second Collect.

O GOD, who for our redemption didst give Thine only begotten Son to the death of the cross; and by His glorious resurrection hast delivered us from the power of our enemy; Grant us so to die daily from sin, that we may evermore live with Him in the joy of His resurrection; through the same Christ our Lord. *Amen.*

The Sentence.

CHRIST being raised from the dead, dieth no more; Death hath no more dominion over Him. *Rom.* 6:9.

Monday in Easter-Week.

The Collect.

O GOD, who hast called us to be children of the resurrection, and hast made us citizens of the Jerusalem which is above; Grant that whensoever in the dimness of this life present our eyes are holden that we see Thee not, our hearts may alway be attentive to Thy holy Word, and burn within us, as it is opened by thy Son, our Saviour Jesus Christ. *Amen.*

The Sentence.

I AM He that liveth, and was dead; and, behold, I am alive for evermore, Amen. *Rev.* 1:18.

Tuesday in Easter-Week.

The Collect.

O HOLY Jesus, who by the travail of Thy soul, hast made a people to be born out of every kindred and nation and tongue; Grant that all those who are called into the unity of Thy Church to be the children of God by the washing of regeneration, may have one faith in their hearts, and one law of holiness in their lives; through Thy merits who livest and reignest with the Father and the Holy Ghost, one God, world without end. *Amen.*

The Sentence.

FOR as in Adam all die, even so in Christ shall all be made alive.
1 *Cor.* 15 : 22.

The First Sunday after Easter.

The Collect.

ALMIGHTY Father, who hast given Thine only Son to die for our sins, and to rise again for our justification; Grant us so to put away the leaven of malice and wickedness, that we may always serve Thee in pureness of living and truth; through the merits of the same Thy Son Jesus Christ our Lord. *Amen.*

The Sentence.

AND this is the record, that God hath given to us eternal life, and this life is in His Son. 1 *St. John* 5:11.

The Second Sunday after Easter.

The Collect.

ALMIGHTY God, who hast given Thine only Son to be unto us both a sacrifice for sin, and also an ensample of godly life; give us grace that we may always most thankfully receive that His inestimable benefit, and also daily endeavor ourselves to follow the blessed steps of His most holy life; through the same Jesus Christ our Lord. *Amen.*

The Sentence.

FOR ye were as sheep going astray; but are now returned unto the Shepherd and Bishop of your souls.
1 *St. Peter* 2:25.

The Third Sunday after Easter.

The Collect.

ALMIGHTY God, who showest to them that are in error the light of Thy truth, to the intent that they may return into the way of righteousness; Grant unto all those who are admitted into the fellowship of Christ's religion, that they may avoid those things that are contrary to their profession, and follow all such things as are agreeable to the same; through our Lord Jesus Christ. *Amen.*

The Sentence.

A LITTLE while, and ye shall not see me: and again, a little while, and ye shall see me, because I go to the Father. *St. John* 16:16.

The Fourth Sunday after Easter.

The Collect.

O ALMIGHTY God, who alone canst order the unruly wills and affections of sinful men; Grant unto Thy people, that they may love the thing which Thou commandest and desire that which Thou dost promise; that so, among the sundry and manifold changes of the world, our hearts may surely there be fixed, where true joys are to be found; through Jesus Christ our Lord. *Amen.*

The Sentence.

IF I go not away, the Comforter will not come unto you; but if I depart, I will send Him unto you.
St. John 16 : 7.

The Fifth Sunday after Easter.

The Collect.

O LORD, from whom all good things do come; Grant to us Thy humble servants, that by Thy holy inspiration we may think those things that are good, and by Thy merciful guiding may perform the same; through our Lord Jesus Christ. *Amen.*

The Sentence.

HITHERTO have ye asked nothing in my Name: ask, and ye shall receive, that your joy may be full.
St. John 16 : 24.

Ascension.

The Ascension-Day.

The Collect.

GRANT, we beseech Thee, Almighty God, that like as we do believe Thy only begotten Son our Lord Jesus Christ to have ascended into the heavens; so we may also in heart and mind thither ascend, and with Him continually dwell, who liveth and reigneth with Thee and the Holy Ghost, one God, world without end. *Amen.*

The Sentence.

LIFT up your heads, O ye gates; and be ye lift up, ye everlasting doors; and the King of glory shall come in.
Ps. 24:7.

Sunday after Ascension-Day.

The Collect.

O GOD the King of glory, who hast exalted Thine only Son Jesus Christ with great triumph unto Thy kingdom in heaven; We beseech Thee, leave us not comfortless; but send to us Thine Holy Ghost to comfort us, and exalt us unto the same place whither our Saviour Christ is gone before, who liveth and reigneth with Thee and the Holy Ghost, one God, world without end. *Amen.*

The Sentence.

WE have a great High Priest, that is passed into the heavens, Jesus the Son of God. *Heb.* 4:14.

Whitsuntide.

Whitsun-Day.

The Collect.

O GOD, who as at this time didst teach the hearts of Thy faithful people, by sending to them the light of Thy Holy Spirit; Grant us by the same Spirit to have a right judgment in all things, and evermore to rejoice in His holy comfort; through the merits of Christ Jesus our Saviour, who liveth and reigneth with Thee, in the unity of the same Spirit, one God, world without end. *Amen.*

The Sentence.

AND suddenly there came a sound from heaven as of a rushing mighty wind, and it filled all the house where they were sitting. *Acts* 2:2.

Whitsun-Day.

The Second Collect.

O GOD, Holy Ghost, who, as on this day, didst descend in the likeness of fiery tongues, bringing to the Church the promise of the Father in the gift of power; Take away all vices from our hearts, and fill us with all wisdom and spiritual understanding. Grant this, O blessed Spirit, who with the Father and the Son, livest and reignest, ever one God, world without end. *Amen.*

The Sentence.

AND they were all filled with the Holy Ghost, and began to speak with other tongues, as the Spirit gave them utterance. *Acts* 2:4.

Monday in Whitsun-Week.

The Collect.

O LORD JESUS CHRIST, who didst send from the Father the Comforter, even the Spirit of Truth; Grant that He may enlighten our minds with the teaching of Thy truth, and sanctify our hearts with the power of Thy grace, so that evermore abiding in Thee we may be found steadfast in faith and holy in life, being conformed unto Thine image, who art with the Father and the Holy Ghost, ever one God, world without end. *Amen.*

The Sentence.

GOD is no respecter of persons: but in every nation he that feareth Him, and worketh righteousness, is accepted with Him. *Acts* 10:34, 35.

Tuesday in Whitsun-Week.

The Collect.

O GOD, the light and life of all believers; Grant that they whom the Holy Ghost hath made Thy children by adoption and grace, loving Thee without lukewarmness, and confessing Thy faith without dissension, may obtain that peace which our Lord Jesus Christ promised to all those who truly follow Him; through the same Jesus Christ our Lord. *Amen.*

The Sentence.

I AM come that they might have life, and that they might have it more abundantly. *St. John* 10 : 10.

Trinity.

Trinity Sunday.

The Collect.

ALMIGHTY and everlasting God, who hast given unto us Thy servants grace, by the confession of a true faith, to acknowledge the glory of the eternal Trinity, and in the power of the Divine Majesty to worship the Unity; We beseech Thee that Thou wouldest keep us steadfast in this faith, and evermore defend us from all adversities, who livest and reignest, one God, world without end. *Amen.*

The Sentence.

THEY rest not day and night, saying, Holy, Holy, Holy, Lord God Almighty, which was, and is, and is to come. *Rev.* 4:8.

The First Sunday after Trinity.

The Collect.

O GOD, the strength of all those who put their trust in Thee; Mercifully accept our prayers: and because, through the weakness of our mortal nature, we can do no good thing without Thee, grant us the help of Thy grace, that in keeping Thy commandments we may please Thee, both in will and deed; through Jesus Christ our Lord. *Amen.*

The Sentence.

GOD is love; and he that dwelleth in love dwelleth in God, and God in him. 1 *St. John* 4:16.

The Second Sunday after Trinity.

The Collect.

O LORD, who never failest to help and govern those whom Thou dost bring up in Thy steadfast fear and love; Keep us, we beseech Thee, under the protection of Thy good providence, and make us to have a perpetual fear and love of Thy holy Name; through Jesus Christ our Lord. *Amen.*

The Sentence.

AND whatsoever we ask, we receive of Him, because we keep His commandments, and do those things which are pleasing in His sight. 1 *St. John* 3 : 22.

The Third Sunday after Trinity.

The Collect.

O LORD, we beseech Thee mercifully to hear us; and grant that we, to whom Thou hast given an hearty desire to pray, may, by Thy mighty aid, be defended and comforted in all dangers and adversities; through Jesus Christ our Lord. *Amen.*

The Sentence.

BE clothed with humility: for God resisteth the proud, and giveth grace to the humble. 1 *St. Peter* 5:5.

The Fourth Sunday after Trinity.

The Collect.

O GOD, the protector of all that trust in Thee, without whom nothing is strong, nothing is holy; Increase and multiply upon us Thy mercy; that, Thou being our ruler and guide, we may so pass through things temporal, that we finally lose not the things eternal. Grant this, O heavenly Father, for Jesus Christ's sake our Lord. *Amen.*

The Sentence.

I RECKON that the sufferings of this present time are not worthy to be compared with the glory which shall be revealed in us. *Rom.* 8:18.

The Fifth Sunday after Trinity.

The Collect.

GRANT, O Lord, we beseech Thee, that the course of this world may be so peaceably ordered by Thy governance, that Thy Church may joyfully serve Thee in all godly quietness; through Jesus Christ our Lord. *Amen.*

The Sentence.

THE eyes of the Lord are over the righteous, and His ears are open unto their prayers. 1 *St. Peter* 3:12.

The Sixth Sunday after Trinity.

The Collect.

O GOD, who hast prepared for those who love Thee such good things as pass man's understanding; Pour into our hearts such love toward Thee, that we, loving Thee above all things, may obtain Thy promises, which exceed all that we can desire; through Jesus Christ our Lord. *Amen.*

The Sentence.

LIKEWISE reckon ye also yourselves to be dead indeed unto sin, but alive unto God through Jesus Christ our Lord. *Rom.* 6:11.

The Seventh Sunday after Trinity.

The Collect.

LORD of all power and might, who art the author and giver of all good things; Graft in our hearts the love of Thy Name, increase in us true religion, nourish us with all goodness, and of Thy great mercy keep us in the same; through Jesus Christ our Lord. *Amen.*

The Sentence.

BUT now being made free from sin, and become servants to God, ye have your fruit unto holiness, and the end everlasting life. *Rom.* 6:22.

The Eighth Sunday after Trinity.

The Collect.

O GOD, whose never-failing providence ordereth all things both in heaven and earth; We humbly beseech Thee, to put away from us all hurtful things, and to give us those things which are profitable for us; through Jesus Christ our Lord. *Amen.*

The Sentence.

THE Spirit itself beareth witness with our Spirit, that we are the children of God. *Rom.* 8:16.

The Ninth Sunday after Trinity.

The Collect.

GRANT to us, Lord, we beseech Thee, the spirit to think and do always such things as are right; that we, who cannot do anything that is good without Thee, may by Thee be enabled to live according to Thy will; through Jesus Christ our Lord. *Amen.*

The Sentence.

FOR they drank of that Spiritual Rock that followed them; and that Rock was Christ. 1 *Cor.* 10:4.

The Tenth Sunday after Trinity.

The Collect.

LET Thy merciful ears, O Lord, be opened to the prayers of Thy humble servants; and that they may obtain their petitions make them to ask such things as shall please Thee; through Jesus Christ our Lord. *Amen.*

The Sentence.

BUT the manifestation of the Spirit is given to every man to profit withal. 1 *Cor.* 12:7.

The Eleventh Sunday after Trinity.

The Collect.

O GOD, who declarest Thy Almighty power chiefly in showing mercy and pity; Mercifully grant unto us such a measure of Thy grace, that we, running the way of Thy commandments, may obtain Thy gracious promises, and be made partakers of Thy heavenly treasure; through Jesus Christ our Lord. *Amen.*

The Sentence.

BY the grace of God I am what I am: and His grace which was bestowed upon me was not in vain. 1 *Cor.* 15:10.

The Twelfth Sunday after Trinity.

The Collect.

ALMIGHTY and everlasting God, who art always more ready to hear than we to pray, and art wont to give more than either we desire or deserve; Pour down upon us the abundance of Thy mercy; forgiving us those things whereof our conscience is afraid, and giving us those good things which we are not worthy to ask, but through the merits and mediation of Jesus Christ, Thy Son, our Lord. *Amen.*

The Sentence.

IF the ministration of condemnation be glory, much more doth the ministration of righteousness exceed in glory. 2 *Cor.* 3 : 9.

The Thirteenth Sunday after Trinity.

The Collect.

ALMIGHTY and merciful God, of whose only gift it cometh that Thy faithful people do unto Thee true and laudable service; Grant, we beseech Thee, that we may so faithfully serve Thee in this life, that we fail not finally to attain Thy heavenly promises; through the merits of Jesus Christ our Lord. *Amen.*

The Sentence.

BUT the Scripture hath concluded all under sin, that the promise by faith of Jesus Christ might be given to them that believe. *Gal.* 3 : 22.

The Fourteenth Sunday after Trinity.

The Collect.

ALMIGHTY and everlasting God, give unto us the increase of faith, hope, and charity; and, that we may obtain that which Thou dost promise, make us to love that which Thou dost command; through Jesus Christ our Lord. *Amen.*

The Sentence.

THE fruit of the Spirit is love, joy, peace, long-suffering, gentleness, goodness, faith, meekness, temperance: against such there is no law.

Gal. 5 : 22, 23.

The Fifteenth Sunday after Trinity.

The Collect.

KEEP, we beseech Thee, O Lord, Thy Church with Thy perpetual mercy; and, because the frailty of man without Thee cannot but fall, keep us ever by Thy help from all things hurtful, and lead us to all things profitable to our salvation; through Jesus Christ our Lord. *Amen.*

The Sentence.

GOD forbid that I should glory, save in the Cross of our Lord Jesus Christ, by whom the world is crucified unto me, and I unto the world.

Gal. 6 : 14.

The Sixteenth Sunday after Trinity.

The Collect.

O LORD, we beseech Thee, let Thy continual pity cleanse and defend Thy Church; and, because it cannot continue in safety without Thy succor, preserve it evermore by Thy help and goodness; through Jesus Christ our Lord. *Amen.*

The Sentence.

NOW unto Him that is able to do exceeding abundantly above all that we ask or think, according to the power that worketh in us, unto Him be glory in the Church by Christ Jesus throughout all ages, world without end. Amen. *Eph.* 3 : 20, 21.

The Seventeenth Sunday after Trinity.

The Collect.

LORD, we pray Thee that Thy grace may always prevent and follow us, and make us continually to be given to all good works; through Jesus Christ our Lord. *Amen.*

The Sentence.

ENDEAVORING to keep the unity of the Spirit in the bond of peace.
Eph. 4 : 3.

The Eighteenth Sunday after Trinity.

The Collect.

LORD, we beseech Thee, grant Thy people grace to withstand the temptations of the world, the flesh, and the devil; and with pure hearts and minds to follow Thee, the only God; through Jesus Christ our Lord. *Amen.*

The Sentence.

WAITING for the coming of our Lord Jesus Christ: who shall also confirm you unto the end. 1 *Cor.* 1 : 7, 8.

The Nineteenth Sunday after Trinity.

The Collect.

O GOD, forasmuch as without Thee we are not able to please Thee; Mercifully grant that Thy Holy Spirit may in all things direct and rule our hearts; through Jesus Christ our Lord. *Amen.*

The Sentence.

AND that ye put on the new man, which after God is created in righteousness and true holiness.

Eph. 4:24.

The Twentieth Sunday after Trinity.

The Collect.

O ALMIGHTY and most merciful God, of Thy bountiful goodness keep us, we beseech Thee, from all things that may hurt us; that we, being ready both in body and soul, may cheerfully accomplish those things which Thou commandest; through Jesus Christ our Lord. *Amen.*

The Sentence.

SPEAKING to yourselves in psalms and hymns and spiritual songs, singing and making melody in your heart to the Lord. *Eph.* 5:19.

The Twenty-first Sunday after Trinity.

The Collect.

GRANT, we beseech Thee, merciful Lord, to Thy faithful people pardon and peace; that they may be cleansed from all their sins, and serve Thee with a quiet mind; through Jesus Christ our Lord. *Amen.*

The Sentence.

WHEREFORE take unto you the whole armor of God, that ye may be able to withstand in the evil day, and having done all, to stand.

Eph. 6:13.

The Twenty-second Sunday after Trinity.

The Collect.

LORD, we beseech Thee to keep Thy household the Church in continual godliness; that through Thy protection it may be free from all adversities, and devoutly given to serve Thee in good works, to the glory of Thy name; through Jesus Christ our Lord. *Amen.*

The Sentence.

BEING confident of this very thing, that He which hath begun a good work in you will perform it until the day of Jesus Christ. *Phil.* 1:6.

The Twenty-third Sunday after Trinity.

The Collect.

O GOD, our refuge and strength, who art the author of all godliness; Be ready, we beseech Thee, to hear the devout prayers of Thy Church; and grant that those things which we ask faithfully we may obtain effectually; through Jesus Christ our Lord. *Amen.*

The Sentence.

FOR our conversation is in heaven; from whence also we look for the Saviour, the Lord Jesus Christ.

Phil. 3:20.

The Twenty-fourth Sunday after Trinity.

The Collect.

O LORD, we beseech Thee, absolve Thy people from their offences; that through Thy bountiful goodness we may all be delivered from the bands of those sins, which by our frailty we have committed. Grant this, O heavenly Father, for Jesus Christ's sake, our blessed Lord and Saviour. *Amen.*

The Sentence.

GIVING thanks unto the Father, which hath made us meet to be partakers of the inheritance of the Saints in light. *Col.* 1 : 12.

The Sunday Next before Advent.

The Collect.

STIR up, we beseech Thee, O Lord, the wills of Thy faithful people; that they, plenteously bringing forth the fruit of good works, may by Thee be plenteously rewarded; through Jesus Christ our Lord. *Amen.*

The Sentence.

AND this is His Name whereby He shall be called, THE LORD OUR RIGHTEOUSNESS. *Jer.* 23:6.

Saints' Days.

Saint Andrew's Day
(November 30).

The Collect.

ALMIGHTY GOD, who didst give such grace unto Thy holy Apostle Saint Andrew, that he readily obeyed the calling of Thy Son Jesus Christ, and followed Him without delay; Grant unto us all, that we, being called by Thy holy Word, may forthwith give up ourselves obediently to fulfill Thy holy commandments; through the same Jesus Christ our Lord. *Amen.*

The Sentence.

FOR with the heart man believeth unto righteousness; and with the mouth confession is made unto salvation. *Rom.* 10 : 10.

Saint Thomas the Apostle
(December 21).

The Collect.

ALMIGHTY and ever-living God, who, for the greater confirmation of the faith, didst suffer Thy holy Apostle Thomas to be doubtful in Thy Son's resurrection; Grant us so perfectly, and without all doubt, to believe in Thy Son Jesus Christ, that our faith in Thy sight may never be reproved. Hear us, O Lord, through the same Jesus Christ, to whom, with Thee and the Holy Ghost, be all honor and glory, now and for evermore. *Amen.*

The Sentence.

BUILT upon the foundation of the Apostles and Prophets, Jesus Christ Himself being the chief cornerstone. *Eph.* 2:20.

The Conversion of Saint Paul
(January 25).

The Collect.

O GOD, who, through the preaching of the blessed Apostle Saint Paul, hast caused the light of the gospel to shine throughout the world; Grant, we beseech Thee, that we, having his wonderful conversion in remembrance, may show forth our thankfulness unto Thee for the same, by following the holy doctrine which he taught; through Jesus Christ our Lord. *Amen.*

The Sentence.

AND he, trembling and astonished said, Lord, what wilt Thou have me to do? *Acts* 9:6.

The Presentation of Christ in the Temple, commonly called, The Purification of Saint Mary the Virgin

(February 2).

The Collect.

ALMIGHTY and ever-living God, we humbly beseech Thy Majesty, that as Thy only-begotten Son was this day presented in the temple in substance of our flesh, so we may be presented unto Thee with pure and clean hearts, by the same Thy Son Jesus Christ our Lord. *Amen.*

The Sentence.

AND when they had performed all things according to the Law of the Lord, they returned into Galilee, to their own city, Nazareth. *St. Luke* 2:39.

Saint Matthias's Day
(February 24).

The Collect.

O ALMIGHTY God, who into the place of the traitor Judas didst choose Thy faithful servant Matthias to be of the number of the twelve Apostles; Grant that Thy Church, being always preserved from false Apostles, may be ordered and guided by faithful and true pastors; through Jesus Christ our Lord. *Amen.*

The Sentence.

AND they gave forth their lots; and the lot fell upon Matthias; and he was numbered with the eleven Apostles.
Acts 1 : 26.

The Annunciation of the Blessed Virgin Mary

(March 25).

The Collect.

WE beseech Thee, O Lord, pour Thy grace into our hearts; that as we have known the incarnation of Thy Son Jesus Christ by the message of an angel, so by His cross and passion we may be brought unto the glory of His resurrection; through the same Jesus Christ our Lord. *Amen.*

The Sentence.

HAIL, thou that art highly favored, the Lord is with thee: Blessed art thou among women. *St. Luke* 1:28.

Saint Mark's Day

(April 25).

The Collect.

O ALMIGHTY God, who hast instructed Thy holy Church with the heavenly doctrine of Thy Evangelist Saint Mark; Give us grace that, being not like children carried away with every blast of vain doctrine, we may be established in the truth of Thy holy Gospel; through Jesus Christ our Lord. *Amen.*

The Sentence.

BUT speaking the truth in love, may grow up into Him in all things, which is the head, even Christ.
Eph. 4:15.

Saint Philip and Saint James's Day
(May 1).

The Collect.

O ALMIGHTY God, whom truly to know is everlasting life; Grant us perfectly to know Thy Son Jesus Christ to be the way, the truth, and the life; that, following the steps of Thy holy Apostles, Saint Philip and Saint James, we may steadfastly walk in the way that leadeth to eternal life; through the same Thy Son Jesus Christ our Lord. *Amen.*

The Sentence.

BUT let patience have her perfect work, that ye may be perfect and entire, wanting nothing.

St. James 1:4.

Saint Barnabas the Apostle
(June 11).

The Collect.

O LORD God Almighty, who didst endue Thy holy Apostle Barnabas with singular gifts of the Holy Ghost; Leave us not, we beseech Thee, destitute of Thy manifold gifts, nor yet of grace to use them alway to Thy honor and glory; through Jesus Christ our Lord. *Amen.*

The Sentence.

WHO, when he came, and had seen the grace of God, was glad, and exhorted them all, that with purpose of heart they would cleave unto the Lord. *Acts* 11:23.

Saint John Baptist's Day

(June 24).

The Collect.

ALMIGHTY God, by whose providence Thy servant John Baptist was wonderfully born, and sent to prepare the way of Thy Son our Saviour, by preaching repentance; Make us so to follow His doctrine and holy life, that we may truly repent according to His preaching; and after His example constantly speak the truth, boldly rebuke vice, and patiently suffer for the truth's sake; through Jesus Christ our Lord. *Amen.*

The Sentence.

PREPARE ye the way of the Lord, make straight in the desert a highway for our God. *Isa.* 40:3.

Saint Peter's Day
(June 29).

The Collect.

O ALMIGHTY God, who by Thy Son Jesus Christ didst give to Thy Apostle Saint Peter many excellent gifts, and commandedst him earnestly to feed Thy flock; Make, we beseech Thee, all Bishops and Pastors diligently to preach Thy holy Word, and the people obediently to follow the same, that they may receive the crown of everlasting glory; through Jesus Christ our Lord. *Amen.*

The Sentence.

AND Simon Peter answered and said, Thou art the Christ, the Son of the living God. *St. Matt.* 16:16.

Saint James the Apostle

(July 25).

The Collect.

GRANT, O merciful God, that as Thine holy Apostle Saint James, leaving his father and all that he had, without delay was obedient unto the calling of Thy Son Jesus Christ, and followed Him; so we, forsaking all worldly and carnal affections, may be evermore ready to follow Thy holy commandments; through Jesus Christ our Lord. *Amen.*

The Sentence.

THE Son of Man came not to be ministered unto, but to minister, and to give His life a ransom for many.

St. Matt. 20: 28.

The Transfiguration of Christ.

(August 6).

The Collect.

O GOD, who on the mount didst reveal to chosen witnesses thine only-begotten Son wonderfully transfigured in raiment white and glistering; Mercifully grant that we, being delivered from the disquietude of this world, may be permitted to behold the King in his beauty, who with Thee, O Father, and Thee, O Holy Ghost, liveth and reigneth one God, world without end. *Amen.*

The Sentence.

AND there came a voice out of the cloud saying, This is my beloved Son, hear him. *St. Luke* 9 : 35.

Saint Bartholomew the Apostle
(August 24).

The Collect.

O ALMIGHTY and everlasting God, who didst give to Thine Apostle Bartholomew grace truly to believe and to preach Thy word; Grant, we beseech Thee, unto Thy Church, to love that word which he believed, and both to preach and receive the same; through Jesus Christ our Lord. *Amen.*

The Sentence.

HE that is greatest among you, let him be as the younger; and he that is chief, as he that doth serve.
St. Luke 22 : 26.

Saint Matthew the Apostle
(September 21).

The Collect.

O ALMIGHTY God, who by Thy blessed Son didst call Matthew from the receipt of custom to be an Apostle and Evangelist; Grant us grace to forsake all covetous desires, and inordinate love of riches, and to follow the same Thy Son Jesus Christ, who liveth and reigneth with Thee and the Holy Ghost, one God, world without end. *Amen.*

The Sentence.

BY manifestation of the truth commending ourselves to every man's conscience in the sight of God.

2 Cor. 4 : 2.

Saint Michael and all Angels
(September 29).

The Collect.

O EVERLASTING God, who hast ordained and constituted the services of Angels and men in a wonderful order; Mercifully grant, that as Thy holy Angels always do Thee service in heaven, so, by Thy appointment, they may succor and defend us on earth; through Jesus Christ our Lord. *Amen.*

The Sentence.

THE chariots of God are twenty thousand, even thousands of Angels; and the Lord is among them as in the holy place of Sinai. *Ps.* 68:17.

Saint Luke the Evangelist
(October 18).

The Collect.

ALMIGHTY God, who calledst Luke the Physician, whose praise is in the Gospel, to be an Evangelist, and Physician of the soul; May it please Thee, that, by the wholesome medicines of the doctrine delivered by him, all the diseases of our souls may be healed; through the merits of Thy Son Jesus Christ our Lord. *Amen.*

The Sentence.

THE Lord appointed other seventy also, and sent them two and two before His face into every city and place, whither He himself would come.

St. Luke 10 : 1.

Saint Simon and Saint Jude, Apostles
(October 28).

The Collect.

O ALMIGHTY God, who hast built Thy Church upon the foundation of the Apostles and Prophets, Jesus Christ himself being the head corner-stone; Grant us so to be joined together in unity of spirit by their doctrine, that we may be made a holy temple acceptable unto Thee; through Jesus Christ our Lord. *Amen.*

The Sentence.

EARNESTLY contend for the faith which was once delivered unto the Saints. *St. Jude* 1:3.

All Saints' Day
(November 1).

The Collect.

O ALMIGHTY God, who hast knit together Thine elect in one communion and fellowship, in the mystical body of Thy Son Christ our Lord; Grant us grace so to follow Thy blessed Saints in all virtuous and godly living, that we may come to those unspeakable joys, which Thou hast prepared for those who unfeignedly love Thee; through Jesus Christ our Lord. *Amen.*

The Sentence.

THE souls of the righteous are in the hand of God, and there shall no torment touch them. In the sight of the unwise, they seemed to die, and their going from us to be utter destruction; but they are in peace. *Wisdom* 13 : 1, 2.

Thanksgiving Day.

The Collect.

O MOST merciful Father, who hast blessed the labors of the husbandman in the returns of the fruits of the earth; we give Thee humble and hearty thanks for this Thy bounty; beseeching Thee to continue Thy loving-kindness to us; that our land may still yield her increase, to Thy glory and our comfort; through Jesus Christ our Lord. *Amen.*

The Sentence.

EVERY good gift and every perfect gift is from above; and cometh down from the Father of Lights, with whom is no variableness, neither shadow of turning. *St. James* 1:17.

Ember Days.

The Collect.

ALMIGHTY God, the giver of all good gifts, who of Thy divine providence hast appointed divers Orders in Thy Church; Give Thy grace, we humbly beseech Thee, to all those who are to be called to any office and administration in the same; and so replenish them with the truth of Thy doctrine, and endue them with innocency of life, that they may faithfully serve before Thee, to the glory of Thy great Name, and the benefit of Thy holy Church; through Jesus Christ our Lord. *Amen.*

The Sentence.

AND He gave some, Apostles; and some, Prophets; and some, Evangelists; and some, Pastors and Teachers; for the perfecting of the Saints, for the work of the Ministry, for the edifying of the Body of Christ. *Eph.* 4:11, 12.

Rogation Days.

The Collect.

ALMIGHTY God, who hast ordained the seed-time and the harvest, we beseech Thee to bless the crops of the field and the kindly fruits of the earth, that the sower may sow in joy and the reapers gather their sheaves in gladness, to the glory of Thy Name, through Jesus Christ our Lord. *Amen.*

The Sentence.

HONOR the Lord with thy substance, and with the first fruits of all thine increase; so shall thy barns be filled with plenty, and thy presses shall burst out with new wine. *Prov.* 3:9, 10.

Occasional Prayers.

From the Communion Office.

ASSIST us mercifully, O Lord, in these our supplications and prayers, and dispose the way of Thy servants towards the attainment of everlasting salvation; that, among all the changes and chances of this mortal life, they may ever be defended by Thy most gracious and ready help; through Jesus Christ our Lord. *Amen.*

From the Communion Office.

GRANT, we beseech Thee, Almighty God, that the words which we have heard this day with our outward ears, may, through Thy grace, be so grafted inwardly in our hearts, that they may bring forth in us the fruit of good living, to the honor and praise of Thy Name; through Jesus Christ our Lord. *Amen.*

DIRECT us, O Lord, in all our doings, with Thy most gracious favor, and further us with Thy continual help; that in all our works begun, continued, and ended in Thee, we may glorify Thy holy Name, and finally, by Thy mercy, obtain everlasting life; through Jesus Christ our Lord. *Amen.*

From the Communion Office.

ALMIGHTY God, the fountain of all wisdom, who knowest our necessities before we ask, and our ignorance in asking; We beseech Thee to have compassion upon our infirmities; and those things, which for our unworthiness we dare not, and for our blindness we cannot ask, vouchsafe to give us, for the worthiness of Thy Son Jesus Christ our Lord. *Amen.*

ALMIGHTY God, who hast promised to hear the petitions of those who ask in Thy Son's Name; We beseech Thee mercifully to incline Thine ears to us who have now made our prayers and supplications unto Thee; and grant, that those things which we have faithfully asked according to Thy will, may effectually be obtained, to the relief of our necessity, and to the setting forth of Thy glory; through Jesus Christ our Lord. *Amen.*

For a Sick Person.

O FATHER of mercies and God of all comfort, our only help in time of need; Look down from heaven, we humbly beseech Thee, behold, visit, and relieve Thy sick *servant*, for whom our prayers are desired. Look upon *him* with the eyes of Thy mercy; comfort *him* with a sense of Thy goodness; preserve *him* from the temptations of the enemy; give *him* patience under *his* affliction; and, in Thy good time, restore *him* to health, and enable *him* to lead the residue of *his* life in Thy fear, and to Thy glory. Or else give *him* grace so to take Thy visitation, that, after this painful life ended, *he* may dwell with Thee in life everlasting; through Jesus Christ our Lord. *Amen.*

For a Sick Child.

ALMIGHTY God, and merciful Father, to whom alone belong the issues of life and death; Look down from heaven, we humbly beseech Thee, with the eyes of mercy, upon the sick *child* for whom our prayers are desired. Deliver *him*, O Lord, in Thy good appointed time, from *his* bodily pain, and visit *him* with Thy salvation; that if it should be Thy good pleasure to prolong *his* days here on earth, *he* may live to Thee, and be an instrument of Thy glory, by serving Thee faithfully, and doing good in *his* generation. Or else receive *him* into those heavenly habitations, where the souls of those who sleep in the Lord Jesus enjoy perpetual rest and felicity. Grant this, O Lord, for the love of Thy Son, our Saviour, Jesus Christ. *Amen.*

Thanksgiving for a Recovery from Sickness.

O GOD, who art the giver of life, of health, and of safety; We bless Thy Name, that Thou hast been pleased to deliver from *his* bodily sickness *this* Thy *servant*, who now *desireth* to return thanks unto Thee, [in the presence of all Thy people.] Gracious art Thou, O Lord, and full of compassion to the children of men. May *his heart* be duly impressed with a sense of Thy merciful goodness, and may *he* devote the residue of *his* days to an humble, holy, and obedient walking before Thee; through Jesus Christ our Lord. *Amen.*

For a Person under Affliction.

O MERCIFUL God, and heavenly Father, who hast taught us in Thy holy Word that Thou dost not willingly afflict or grieve the children of men; Look with pity, we beseech Thee, upon the sorrows of Thy *servant*, for whom our prayers are desired. In Thy wisdom Thou hast seen fit to visit *him* with trouble, and to bring distress upon *him*. Remember *him*, O Lord, in mercy; sanctify Thy fatherly correction to *him*; endue *his* soul with patience under *his* affliction, and with resignation to Thy blessed will; comfort *him* with a sense of Thy goodness; lift up Thy countenance upon *him*, and give *him* peace; through Jesus Christ our Lord. *Amen.*

For our Loved Ones in Paradise.

ALMIGHTY God, with whom do live the spirits of those who depart hence in the Lord, and with whom the souls of the faithful, after they are delivered from the burden of the flesh, are in joy and felicity; We give Thee hearty thanks for the good examples of all those Thy servants, who, having finished their course in faith, do now rest from their labors. And we beseech Thee, that we, with all those who are departed in the true faith of Thy holy Name, may have our perfect consummation and bliss, both in body and soul, in Thy eternal and everlasting glory; through Jesus Christ our Lord. *Amen.*

From the Visitation Office.

O GOD, whose days are without end, and whose mercies cannot be numbered; Make us, we beseech Thee, deeply sensible of the shortness and uncertainty of human life; and let Thy Holy Spirit lead us through this vale of misery, in holiness and righteousness, all the days of our lives: That, when we shall have served Thee in our generation, we may be gathered unto our fathers, having the testimony of a good conscience; in the communion of the catholic Church; in the confidence of a certain faith; in the comfort of a reasonable, religious, and holy hope; in favor with Thee our God, and in perfect charity with the world. All which we ask through Jesus Christ our Lord. *Amen.*

For a Person, or Persons, going to Sea.

O ETERNAL God, who alone spreadest out the heavens, and rulest the raging of the sea; We commend to Thy Almighty protection, Thy *servant*, for whose preservation on the great deep our prayers are desired. Guard *him*, we beseech Thee, from the dangers of the sea, from sickness, from the violence of enemies, and from every evil to which *he* may be exposed. Conduct *him* in safety to the haven where *he* would be, with a grateful sense of Thy mercies; through Jesus Christ our Lord. *Amen.*

Thanksgiving for a safe return from Sea.

MOST gracious Lord, whose mercy is over all Thy works; We praise Thy holy Name that Thou hast been pleased to conduct in safety through the perils of the great deep, *this* Thy *servant*, who now *desireth* to return *his* thanks to Thee. May *he* be duly sensible of Thy merciful providence towards *him*, and ever express *his* thankfulness by a holy trust in Thee and obedience to Thy laws; through Jesus Christ our Lord. *Amen.*

For Missions.

O GOD, who hast made of one blood all nations of men for to dwell on the face of the whole earth, and didst send Thy blessed Son to preach peace to them that are far off and them that are nigh; Grant that all men everywhere may seek after Thee and find Thee. Be graciously pleased to multiply and bless the heralds of the Gospel of Thy Son; and shortly to accomplish the number of Thine elect, and to hasten Thy kingdom; through the same Jesus Christ our Lord. *Amen.*

For the Increase of the Ministry.

O LORD Jesus Christ, who didst command Thy disciples to pray the Lord of the harvest that He would send forth laborers into His harvest; we beseech Thee graciously to increase the number of faithful ministers of Thy Word and Sacraments, and to send them forth among all nations of men; that perishing souls may be saved, and the bounds of Thy blessed kingdom be enlarged. We ask it, O merciful Saviour, for the glory of Thy Name, who livest and reignest with the Father and the Holy Ghost, one God, world without end. *Amen.*

For the Birthday of a Child.

O GOD, who hast taught us that they who seek Thee early shall find Thee; Grant unto this, Thy child, that, as *he* increases in stature, *he* may also increase in wisdom and in favor with God and man; through Jesus Christ our Lord. *Amen.*

For the Birthday of an Adult.

O GOD, who art the author of our being, and whose providence has added another year to the life of Thy servant; Teach *him* so to number *his* days, that *he* may apply *his* heart unto wisdom; through Jesus Christ our Lord. *Amen.*

For the Family.

O ETERNAL Father, who hast promised Thy blessing to the Families that call upon Thy Name, grant Thy blessing to this Household, that every member of the same may faithfully serve Thee. Give unto the Parents grace, both by precept and example, to train up their children in the fear of the Lord; may the children be faithful to their Baptismal vows as members of Thy Mystical Body; and may we all, as a Christian Family, serve Thee in a loving, trustful, and faithful obedience; through Jesus Christ our Lord. *Amen.*

For the Minister and Congregation.

GRANT, O Lord, that Thy servant, who ministers to us in holy things, may be enabled so to dispense the mysteries of Thy grace and truth that we, who are committed to his spiritual care, may be built up in our most holy faith and perfected in the energies of a loving obedience; through Thy Son Jesus Christ our Lord. *Amen.*

For the Rector and Parish.

O LORD Jesus Christ, who hast sent Thy ministers before Thee to prepare Thy way, grant to Thy servant (N. . . . .), the Rector of this Parish, all wisdom and strength needful for his holy task: and may all the members of his Parish both enjoy the benefit of his ministrations and co-operate with him in advancing Thy kingdom, who livest and reignest with the Father and the Holy Ghost, ever one God, world without end. *Amen.*

For the Bishop and Diocese.

ALMIGHTY and Everlasting God, from whom cometh every good and perfect gift; send down upon our Bishop and other clergy, and upon the congregations committed to their charge, the healthful spirit of Thy grace; and that they may truly please Thee, pour upon them the continual dew of Thy blessing. Grant this, O Lord, for the honor of our Advocate and Mediator, Jesus Christ. *Amen.*

For the Church in our own Land.

DISSIPATE, we meekly beseech Thee, O Lord Jesus Christ, every self-willed opinion which tends by subversion of the faith to counteract the truth; that as Thou art acknowledged in heaven and in earth to be the one and only God, so Thy people, gathered from all nations, may glorify Thee in the unity of the faith handed down from the beginning. *Amen.*

For the Church Militant.

O ETERNAL God and merciful Father, we humbly pray for Thy Holy Church throughout the world, that, it being purged from false philosophy and vain deceit, we may live and act as befits the members of the mystical Body of Thy Son, and in the end be found acceptable unto Thee; through the same Jesus Christ our Lord. *Amen.*

For Christian Unity.

O LORD Jesus Christ, who saidst unto Thine Apostles, Peace I leave with you, My peace I give unto you; regard not our sins, but the faith of Thy Holy Church, and grant her that peace and unity which is agreeable to Thy will, Who livest and reignest for ever and ever. *Amen.*

New Year's Day
(January 1).

O ALMIGHTY God, to whom a thousand years are but as a single day, grant to us, Thy children, that we may so spend the years of our mortal life in Thy service that we may finally attain to the life eternal which Thou hast promised us, in Jesus Christ our Lord. *Amen.*

Washington's Birthday
(February 22).

O ALMIGHTY God, who dost order the affairs of men and nations, make us, we beseech Thee, deeply sensible of Thy mercy in raising up for us a Leader, to be the Father of his country; may we ever remember both his patriotism and his pious devotion as a member of Thy Holy Church; and enable us to shew forth our gratitude for Thy goodness by the faithful discharge of our duties as citizens and by an humble and obedient following of Thee; through Jesus Christ our Lord. *Amen.*

Arbor Day.

O ETERNAL Father, who didst place our first parents in the midst of a garden, and who hast revealed Thy perfect redemption of mankind in the tree of life, whose leaves are for the healing of the nations, bless, we beseech Thee, our efforts this day, and may the shade and substance of the trees we plant be a comfort and blessing to future generations; through Jesus Christ our Lord. *Amen.*

Decoration Day

(May 30).

O GOD, who hast inspired Thy servants to lay down their lives for the preservation of the liberties of our native land, grant that we may ever remember the holy sacrifice which they have made for us, and as we decorate their graves with flowers, help us to emulate their heroic patriotism and to be true and faithful to the privileges which they have purchased for us by their death; through Jesus Christ our Lord. *Amen.*

Independence Day

(July 4).

O GOD, who art the Ruler of nations and the Governor of the whole earth, accept, we beseech Thee, our thanksgiving for the blessings which Thou hast conferred upon us as a Nation; for the courage of those who inaugurated its History; for the Providential goodness which guided its early struggles for Independence, and for the civil Liberty which Thou hast bestowed upon us as a People; through Jesus Christ our Lord. *Amen.*

Labor Day.

O ETERNAL Father, who hast ordained that the workman is worthy of his hire, give to both employers and employed the spirit of mutual confidence and fraternal regard, so that, recognizing their several responsibilities, they may labor together in the sacred union of one common fellowship and brotherhood in Jesus Christ our Lord. *Amen.*

Election Day.

O ETERNAL Father, who in Thy Providence hast committed to each of us a share in the control of our Government, grant, we beseech Thee, that we may so discharge the duty of our citizenship that we may obtain Thy approval and contribute to the welfare of our Nation, in all godliness and true holiness; through Jesus Christ our Lord. *Amen.*

A Morning Prayer.

O GOD, the King eternal, who dividest the day from the darkness, and turnest the shadow of death into the morning; Drive far off from us all wrong desires, incline our hearts to keep Thy law, and guide our feet into the way of peace, that having done Thy will with cheerfulness while it was day, we may, when the night cometh, rejoice to give Thee thanks; through Jesus Christ our Lord. *Amen.*

An Evening Prayer.

O LORD our God, who alone makest us to dwell in safety; Refresh with quiet sleep, this night, those who are wearied with the labors of the day; and mercifully protect from harm all who put their trust in Thee; that lying down in peace to take our rest, we may fear no evil, but confidently give ourselves into Thy holy keeping; through Jesus Christ our Lord. *Amen.*

A Prayer of Saint Chrysostom.

ALMIGHTY God, who hast given us grace at this time with one accord to make our common supplications unto Thee; and dost promise that when two or three are gathered together in Thy Name thou wilt grant their requests; Fulfill now, O Lord, the desires and petitions of Thy servants, as may be most expedient for them; granting us in this world knowledge of Thy truth, and in the world to come life everlasting. *Amen.*

2 Cor. 13 : 14.

THE grace of our Lord Jesus Christ, and the love of God, and the fellowship of the Holy Ghost, be with us all evermore. *Amen.*

Grace at Table.

V. The eyes of all wait upon Thee, O Lord;
R. And Thou givest them their meat in due season.
V. Thou openest Thine hand;
R. And fillest all things living with plenteousness.

And this:

GRANT us Thy blessing with these Thy gifts, O Lord; and feed our souls with the bread of life; through Jesus Christ our Saviour. *Amen.*

Or this:

BLESS, O Lord, these Thy gifts to our use; and make us thankful for Christ's sake. *Amen.*

The Beatitudes of the Gospel.

The Beatitudes of the Gospel.

St. Matt. 5:3-12.

BLESSED are the poor in spirit:
For theirs is the kingdom of heaven.
Blessed are they that mourn:
For they shall be comforted.
Blessed are the meek:
For they shall inherit the earth.
Blessed are they which do hunger and thirst after righteousness:
For they shall be filled.
Blessed are the merciful:
For they shall obtain mercy.
Blessed are the pure in heart:
For they shall see God.
Blessed are the peace-makers:
For they shall be called the children of God.

Blessed are they which are persecuted for righteousness' sake:
For theirs is the kingdom of heaven.
Blessed are ye when men shall revile you, and persecute you, and shall say all manner of evil against you falsely, for my sake.
Rejoice and be exceeding glad: for great is your reward in heaven; for so persecuted they the prophets which were before you.

The Summary of the Law.

The Summary of the Law.

THOU shalt love the Lord thy God with all thy heart, and with all thy soul, and with all thy mind. This is the first and great commandment. And the second is like unto it: Thou shalt love thy neighbor as thyself. On these two commandments hang all the Law and the Prophets. *St. Matt.* 22 : 37–41.

Even Song.

Even Song.

In the Name of the Father, and of the Son, and of the Holy Ghost.

A - men.

I will lay me down in peace and take my... rest.

204   FAMILY PRAYERS

R. For it is Thou, Lord, only that makest me......... dwell in safety.

V. Let my prayer be set forth in Thy sight.......... as the | incense.
R. And the lifting up of my hands as an........... eve - ning | sacrifice.

V. Praise ye the Lord.

R. The Lord's name be prais - ed.

FAMILY PRAYERS

Glory be to the Father, and to the Son, and to the Holy Ghost;

As it was in the beginning, is... now, and ever shall be world with-out end. A-men.

The Apostles' Creed.

FAMILY PRAYERS 207

R. And grant us Thy sal - va - tion.

V. O God, make clean our hearts within us.

R. And take not Thy Ho - ly Spir-it from us.

Our Father, who art in heaven, &c.

Amens.

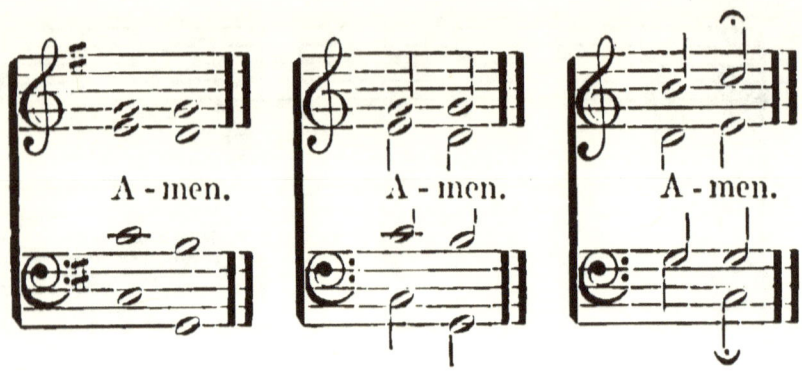

After "The grace of our Lord."

www.ingramcontent.com/pod-product-compliance
Lightning Source LLC
Chambersburg PA
CBHW031824230426

43669CB00009B/1216